My Science Library

Natural or Man-Made?

by Kelli Hicks

Science Content Editor:
Kristi Lew

Rourke
Educational Media

rourkeeducationalmedia.com

Science content editor: Kristi Lew
A former high school teacher with a background in biochemistry and more than 10 years of experience in cytogenetic laboratories, Kristi Lew specializes in taking complex scientific information and making it fun and interesting for scientists and non-scientists alike. She is the author of more than 20 science books for children and teachers.

www.rourkeeducationalmedia.com

Photo credits: Cover © mycola, Tischenko Irina, Cover logo frog © Eric Pohl, test tube © Sergey Lazarev; Table Of Contents © Granite; Page 4 © IKO; Page 5 © Jaimie Duplass; Page 7 © Kevin Eaves; Page 9 © shirophoto; Page 10 © Juriah Mosin; Page 11 © Ewa Walicka; Page 12 © Neeila; Page 13 © Alexanderus; Page 14 © Dmitri Melnik; Page 15 © Granite; Page 16 © CREATISTA; Page 17 © Aleksandr Bryliaev; Page 18 © eans; Page 19 © Yossi Manor; Page 20 © Zeljko Radojko; Page 21 © Alexey Antipov

Editor: Jeanne Sturm

Cover and page design by Nicola Stratford, bdpublishing.com

Library of Congress Cataloging-in-Publication Data

Hicks, Kelli L.
 Natural or man-made? / Kelli Hicks.
    p. cm. -- (My science library)
 Includes bibliographical references and index.
 ISBN 978-1-61741-756-6 (Hard cover) (alk. paper)
 ISBN 978-1-61741-958-4 (Soft cover)
 1. Materials--Juvenile literature. 2. Synthetic products--Juvenile literature. 3. Raw materials--Juvenile literature. 4. Natural resources--Juvenile literature. I. Title. II. Series.

TA403.2.H53 2012
670--dc22

                              2011004843

Rourke Educational Media
Printed in the United States of America,
North Mankato, Minnesota

rourkeeducationalmedia.com

customerservice@rourkeeducationalmedia.com • PO Box 643328 Vero Beach, Florida 32964

Table of Contents

Think About It

Take a drink of water. Play a game on the computer. Have you thought about where the water came from or how the computer was made? Everything in our world is either natural or man-made.

Water travels from a natural source through man-made pipes to get to the water fountain.

5

Is It Natural or Man-Made?

What makes something natural? Think of the things that come directly from the **environment**. Air, water, and soil are resources that exist in nature. People cannot make **natural resources**.

People need to protect our natural resources because they can not be replaced.

People can change natural resources. Something created by a person that does not occur naturally in the environment is man-made. Let's see if we can decide what is natural and what is man-made.

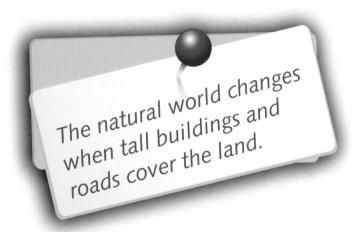

The natural world changes when tall buildings and roads cover the land.

Take a walk outside. Breathe in the fresh air and look around. Do you see any trees? The air is natural and so are the trees.

People use the trees to make new things. Trees are cut down to make **lumber** to build houses. We can also change trees into paper. Paper is man-made.

When you visit the beach, you can feel the sand between your toes. Nobody makes the sand, it occurs naturally in the environment. Some people use the sand to make glass bottles or jars. A glass bottle or jar is man-made.

Heavy machines dig below the top layers of rock to uncover the limestone beneath.

Have you ever heard of **limestone**? It is a type of rock that occurs naturally in the environment. We dig limestone from the Earth and use it as stones for buildings. We also use limestone to make toothpaste. Toothpaste is man-made.

An artist uses his hands and a spinning pottery wheel to change the shape of the clay.

Clay also comes from nature. It comes from finely ground **minerals**. People mold clay into plates, pots for plants, and floor tiles. Clay **pottery** is man-made.

Food for Thought

Many living things eat fruit and vegetables. Fruit and vegetables are natural. Did you know that people use carrots, **avocados**, grapes, and even cucumbers to make other things? People use them to make shampoo and skin lotion. Shampoo and lotion are both man-made.

People can use natural ingredients to make products that heal the body or keep it healthy.

20

Wheat is a type of grass found in many parts of the world. Wheat is natural. We use it to make cereal and flour. We also weave it into baskets or mats. Cereal, flour, baskets, and mats are all man-made.

Natural whole grain used to make cereal provides good nutrition.

SHOW What You Know

1. How do you know if something is natural or if it is man-made?

2. What are some uses for limestone?

3. How can fruit and vegetables be used for something other than food?

Glossary

avocados (av-uh-KAH-doz): green or black pear-shaped fruit with tough skin and creamy, light green pulp

environment (en-VYE-ruhn-muhnt): the natural world of the land, sea, and air

limestone (LIME-stohn): a hard rock used in building and making lime and cement

lumber (LUHM-bur): wood or timber that has been sawed

minerals (MIN-ur-uhlz): substances found in nature that are not animals or plants, such as quartz and pumice

natural resources (NACH-ur-uhl REE-sorsez): material produced by the Earth that is useful to people

pottery (POT-ur-ee): objects made of baked clay

Websites

www.kids.niehs.nih.gov/recycle.htm

www.dnr.wi.gov/eek/

www.brainpop.com/science/

www.rocksforkids.com/RFK/identification.html

www.neok12.com/Natural-Resources.htm

About the Author

Kelli Hicks is a writer, reader, and admirer of the beauty of nature. Even so, she would be lost without her man-made laptop computer. She lives in Tampa, Florida, with her husband, her children Mackenzie and Barrett, and their golden retriever Gingerbread.